Mysterious You

Achoo!

The most interesting book you'll ever read about germs

Written by Trudee Romanek

Illustrated by Rose Cowles

SCHOLASTIC INC.
New York Toronto London Auckland Sydney
Mexico City New Delhi Hong Kong Buenos Aires

For Scott, my sniffler — T.R.

Special thanks to Dorothy Crawford, professor of medical microbiology at the University of Edinburgh,
who was kind enough to review and comment on the contents of this book early in its development.
Thanks also to Dr. Greg Bossart of the Harbor Branch Oceanographic Institute in Fort Pierce,
Florida, and to my editor, Liz MacLeod, for always pointing me in the right direction.
And to Marie and Rose, thanks for making the book look so fabulous!

Edited by Elizabeth MacLeod. Designed by Marie Bartholomew.

ISBN-13: 978-0-545-10593-4
ISBN-10: 0-545-10593-5

8 9 10 11 12 13 14 15   08   18 17 16 15 14 13

Contents

Fighting Germs for Life

Everybody sneezes. But no one sneezes like Donna Griffiths of Worcester, England. She began sneezing on January 13, 1981, when she was 12 and just kept going. Donna sneezed once every minute for days and days. A year later, she'd sneezed about a million times.

Eventually, Donna's sneezes slowed down to one every five minutes or so. And then, finally, on September 16, 1983, she celebrated her first day without a single sneeze. By then she'd been sneezing for 978 days — almost three years.

Why Donna sneezed for so long is a mystery her doctors couldn't explain. Usually sneezes are a sign that there's something in your nose and your body wants to get rid of it. Without even thinking, you take in a big breath and blast it through your nose and mouth, spraying out whatever germs, dust or other particles tickled your nose in the first place.

Sneezing's just one part of your body's defense system — a system working to protect you from germs that can make you mildly sick or dangerously ill. But sneezing isn't the only way your body can clean up its act. Did you know you have a whole army of defenders fighting off germs? Without them, your life would be just one sickness after another.

- It's impossible to keep your eyes open while you sneeze.

- When you sneeze, air and particles leave your mouth and nose at about 150 km/h (93 m.p.h.).

- People used to think that if you didn't cover your nose and mouth when you sneezed, your soul might escape. That's why, when you sneeze, some people say "Bless you." Others say "GESUNDHEIT," which means "good health" in German.

The Bubble Boy

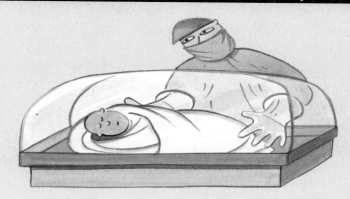

Imagine living your whole life inside just one room. David Vetter did. In 1971, David was born with something called Severe Combined Immune Deficiency, or SCID. His body couldn't fight off germs and disease.

To keep all germs away from him, doctors placed David, just seconds old, inside a germ-free incubator. Later he moved into a germ-free plastic room — a "bubble" with clear plastic walls. David was fine for 12 years until doctors tried a bone-marrow transplant to cure him. Germs in the marrow made David sick, and he died a few months later from the sickness his body couldn't defeat.

Luckily, David's bubble was the first and last of its kind. Now, when doctors discover SCID in a very young baby, they can strengthen the immune system and give the child a better, healthier life.

Teeny Tag-Alongs

Away back in 1674, a frog helped Antoni van Leeuwenhoek of Holland make an incredible discovery. Van Leeuwenhoek was an amateur scientist so fascinated by microscopes that he'd built some of his own. One rainy day, as he went for a walk, a leaping frog drew his attention to a puddle.

Van Leeuwenhoek collected a drop of puddle water and put it under a microscope. He was amazed to see a whole community of creatures swimming in this one drop — tiny beings no one had ever seen before.

These tiny beings, called microbes, are everywhere: in dirt, in food and on your kitchen table. People are covered in them, too. There are more microbes on your body and inside it than there are people in the world — more than 6 BILLION.

Microbes can't survive on their own. They need food. Once they settle into a home — you, for instance — they steal vitamins and other nutrients and leave behind dead cells and poisonous liquids called toxins. Some microbes can make you sick. People usually call these ones germs. Luckily for you, there are more harmless ones than bad ones.

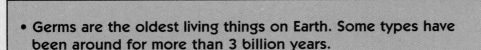

- **Germs are the oldest living things on Earth. Some types have been around for more than 3 billion years.**

- **Mushrooms between your toes? Athlete's foot, the world's most common skin infection, is a type of fungus, just like mushrooms. Almost all of us get infected with this germ at least once in our life.**

Germ ID

There are four main kinds of germs — bacteria, viruses, fungi (FUNG-guy) and protozoa. Bacteria and viruses are the two that most often make people sick. Bacteria move in and treat your body like a giant banquet, munching on whatever parts of you they like. Viruses use a different kind of attack. They take over your cells and force them to make more and more viruses.

You Try It

Find out if there really are germs on your hands. Don't wash them first — that would be cheating. You'll need an adult to help you with the cooking part.

1. Boil 250 mL (1 c.) of water in a small pot. Add two envelopes of unflavored gelatin and one beef bouillon cube or packet. Stir to dissolve.

2. Boil gently for half an hour. Stir every few minutes.

3. Pour into a clean, shallow container and refrigerate.

4. In an hour or two, when the gelatin has set completely, press your hand firmly against it. Cover the dish with clear plastic. NOW you can wash your hands.

5. Set in a dark place at room temperature for five days.

The specks you see on your gelatin are clusters of germs — probably fungi. They grew from the germs on your hand that stuck to the gelatin when you pressed against it. Don't forget to scrape your experiment, still covered with plastic, into the garbage. And wash your hands again.

Greedy Gobblers

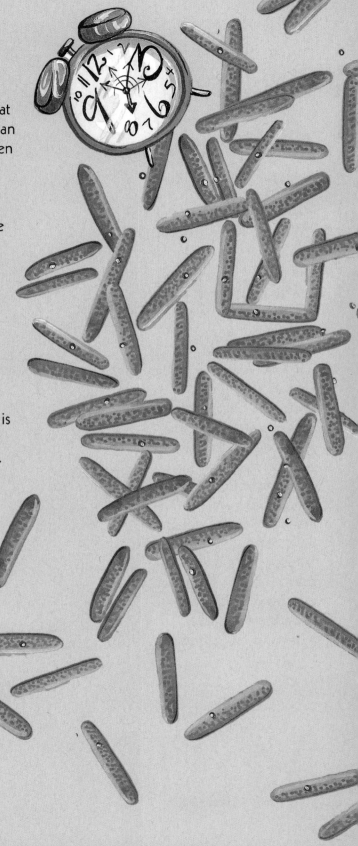

Like all germs, bacteria are VERY small. A cluster of one million of them is only the size of a pinprick. But that doesn't mean they're an easy enemy to fight off. They can be really powerful because they're such great eaters, even though they don't have stomachs or mouths.

To eat, each one — called a bacterium — swims around in your body fluids, soaking up dissolved food and nutrients through holes in its skin, the way a sponge soaks up spills. Then it swims off to find more.

Some bacteria even give off poisons, or toxins, that kill a tiny part of your body. The toxins break down that part into smaller bites that they can slurp up along with the other nutrients.

Bacteria inside you can cause all sorts of problems. Strep throat, ear infections and whooping cough are all caused by bacteria. So are tetanus, tuberculosis and bacterial pneumonia (noo-MO-nya).

Your body could handle a few bacteria. The trouble is that these germs are great at multiplying. Each bacterium gets bigger and, every 20 minutes or so, splits into two. Each of those grows and splits. Then those four split into eight, and so on, until, just eight hours later, your body has almost 17 million of these tiny enemies to deal with.

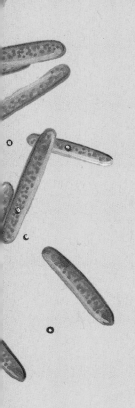

- You have approximately 400 types of harmless bacteria in your colon, or lower intestine. These bacteria and others in your stomach and small intestine help break down tough foods.

- If they get mixed into food or water, some bad bacteria, such as salmonella and E. coli, can cause food poisoning.

- Not all bacteria are bad. Some compost kitchen waste; others make yogurt and cheese. Each spoonful of some types of yogurt contains about 10 million live bacteria.

Real-Life Horror Story

On January 24, 1996, Donna Batdorff got sick. Really sick. What she thought was the flu turned out to be necrotizing fasciitis (fa-shee-EYE-tis) — flesh-eating bacteria. These nasty little germs got into her body through a small cut on one finger and spread like crazy.

As the bacteria grew and spread, they gobbled up flesh on her fingers and arm. As well, the toxins they produced to break down their "food" were poisoning the rest of Donna. Doctors had to work fast. By the time they had the disease under control, Donna had lost parts of four fingers and needed skin grafts to cover the bare muscles left on her arm, but she was alive. Luckily, this horrifying sickness is very rare.

Even Smaller Enemies

You may never have gotten sick from bacteria, but EVERYBODY has had a virus. Every cold and every case of flu is caused by tiny little virus particles.

A virus particle is a sort of coded message inside a package. Each type of virus package has certain chemicals on its surface that can attach only to specific cells in your body, kind of like two puzzle pieces fitting together, or a key sliding into a lock.

Once the package is attached to your cell, the message slips inside. It tells the cell to stop working for your body and instead to make more virus packages, each with the same message.

The cell makes hundreds of new packages. Then these burst out and drift to other cells, which make more packages, and so on. The body cells they leave behind are usually dead or very weak.

Flu viruses are quick-change artists. Every once in a while, they change their message just a little, like a bad guy who gets his hair cut so he won't be recognized. That's how a flu virus keeps going. It changes just enough that scientists can't come up with medicine that'll get rid of it.

Mumps, measles, chicken pox, AIDS and rabies are all caused by viruses. So are other illnesses you might not have heard of, such as hepatitis, poliomyelitis (polio), mononucleosis and yellow fever.

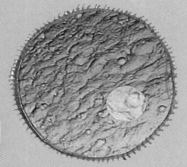

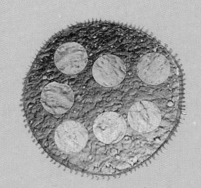

What's the Difference?

Viruses and bacteria are both microscopic germs, but they're different in many ways. Bacteria are like tiny animals — they can move around, and they can reproduce. Viruses aren't anything like animals. Some scientists don't think viruses are even alive. A virus can't reproduce or move without help. It has to hang out waiting to be swept along by a sneeze or a wave of body fluid.

Which are more dangerous? Viruses and bacteria can both be deadly, but in a battle between the two, certain viruses win. They're so small they can get inside bacteria and make THEM sick.

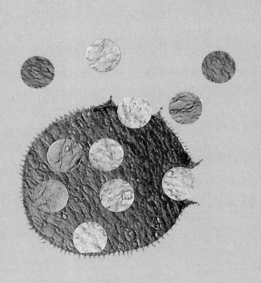

Good Guy Viruses

- **Most cold and flu viruses get in through your nose or your tear ducts — almost never through your mouth.**

- **Viruses are much tinier than bacteria. If the average virus was the size of a baseball, the average bacterium would be as big as the pitcher's mound.**

Researchers have found a way to turn virus enemies into allies. They've created a herpes simplex virus — the kind that causes cold sores — that will invade only cells that are growing and dividing quickly.

When researchers inject this virus into a cancerous tumor in a person's brain, the virus heads straight for the fast-growing cancer cells. It ignores the healthy brain cells because they don't divide at all. As the viruses do their thing, the cancer cells get killed. Researchers are experimenting with other ways viruses might be able to help people, too.

Germs Get Around

Even though scientists first saw microbes in 1674, they didn't realize for about two hundred years that these germs could make people sick. People had all kinds of weird ideas about why we get sick.

Doctors thought poisonous gas from earthquakes or volcanoes spread sickness through the air. In Italy, people thought their health was influenced by the position of the stars and planets. (The Italian word "influenza" is what gave the flu its name.) A cold was called a cold because people thought you could catch one if you let yourself get chilled.

Finally, sometime in the 1880s, French chemist Louis Pasteur did some experiments and realized it was tiny living bacteria that were making people sick. More scientists ran experiments and realized that other, even smaller creatures — viruses — caused illness too.

Pasteur also realized that germs from one person could make another sick. He convinced doctors to wash their hands and instruments so they wouldn't spread illness from one patient to others they touched.

- **Don't Feed the Animals!** Gorillas and other zoo animals that have a lot in common with people can get very sick from germs on snacks tossed to them by human visitors.

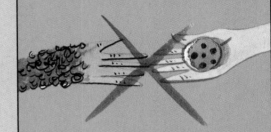

- **People in Antarctica don't get many colds.** That's because the viruses that cause them can't survive long enough in the frigid air to get from one person to another.

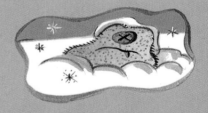

- A housefly can carry germs a distance of up to 24 km (15 mi.).

It's Spreading!

Cold and flu viruses spread very easily. Say your sister has the flu. If she sneezes, you might breathe in the germs she has just sprayed into the air. Or, she might cough germs into her hand and spread them to everything she touches: doorknobs, faucets, the telephone, the computer mouse, towels. And those germs can survive there for three hours.

Then you come along and put your hand on that same doorknob. Now YOUR hand is covered in flu germs. Before you know it, you've rubbed your eye or your nose and those germs are inside you.

Next time you feel a sneeze coming on, use a tissue and then wash your hands. Or, if there's no time, cover up with your shirt sleeve. Any germs you spray will die there instead of traveling on from your hand to the doorknob and then to someone else's hand.

Germ Zone!

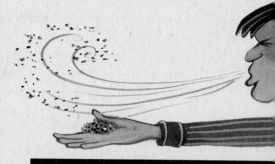

How far can a sneeze spread germs? Try this glitter experiment to see. Go outside and pour a small mound of glitter on the flat palm of your hand. Now, take a deep breath and aim your best fake sneeze right into the glitter. Watch how far and wide it spreads. When a real sneeze comes blasting out your schnozz, it can send germs up to 9 m (30 ft.) away.

Zits, Pits and Bad Breath

In 1999, a Japanese electronics company began selling a small device that can detect smelly breath. You blow into it, and it measures the gases in your mouth that cause bad breath. In the first year alone, the company sold 800,000 of them. What causes this stinky problem everyone wants to get rid of? Bacteria.

Millions of bacteria in your mouth—about 80 kinds—snack on leftover food and give off an acid that eats holes, or cavities, in your teeth. These bacteria also give off gases that smell terrible. Flossing and brushing clean out most of them and leave little food for any you missed.

Even outside your body, bacteria can be a real pain. They can get stuck in the tiny holes, or pores, of your skin and give you pimples. Another type of bacteria in your eyes can cause a painful infection called pinkeye.

Bacteria also cause body odor. Once you hit puberty, your armpits and other parts start to sweat more of a liquid that the bacteria on your skin love. As they gobble it up, they give off waste products that stink. And then you stink too.

The best way to foil these smelly pests is to keep your body clean. Regular showers wash away many of the bacteria that cause the problem. And don't forget to wash your clothes, too, to get rid of the bacteria there.

- Cold sores are caused by viruses that hang around harmlessly in your skin cells and then suddenly flare up, especially when you're overtired or stressed. Warts are viruses in your skin, too, but no one's sure yet what triggers them to pop out.

- Whiteheads are caused by bacteria. If you squeeze one, the bacteria inside could spread under the skin and cause more pimples.

Down the Drain

There are so many germs on Earth that, together, they weigh more than all the living animals and plants combined. Everything you touch has germs on it. No wonder your parents are always nagging you to wash your hands. It's a great defense if you do it right. That means coating your hands in suds and scrubbing everything—fingernails, between your fingers, the backs of your hands, too—for 30 seconds (about as long as it takes to sing "Happy Birthday" twice). The soap and the rubbing loosen the germs from your skin.

Lots of soaps now have anti-bacterials—special ingredients that kill many germs instead of just washing them away. Sounds great, but is it really? Some experts say that regular soap is all you need if you wash properly. They worry that the germs that survive might turn into "superbugs" that aren't damaged at all by antibacterials or by the antibiotics doctors use to help patients get rid of bacteria.

Battling the Bad Guys

How would you keep people out of a top-secret building? Build fences around it? Put up security cameras to keep watch? You might even hire guards. Your body has similar defenses against germs that try to get in.

Think of your skin as a big fence. It surrounds almost your whole body and is thick enough to keep germs out. Some places on your body — such as your eyes, your mouth and your nose — might seem like big open doorways germs could walk right through. But even there, your body has a security system.

You have eyebrows, eyelashes and eyelids to block bits that might fall into your eyes. Your nose hairs protect your nose in the same way. Your lips can seal your mouth up fairly tight. And your ears have tiny hairs, as well as sticky wax — called cerumen (si-ROO-men) — to trap anything that doesn't belong there.

These security features are part of what's called your immune system. A big part of its job is to keep germs out so you stay healthy.

It's Infected!

If you've ever had a cut that got more red and puffy instead of getting better, it may have been infected. Bacteria from the outside got through to the inside. And that's not good.

Usually, your body can clear up a small infection with no trouble. Bacteria that get far inside a person's body, though, through a deep cut or a surgical incision, can cause serious problems and even death if they're not cleaned out.

- **In medieval times, ear wax was mixed into the inks that were used to decorate parchments.**

You Try It

Your skin's a lot like the skin of an apple: both are great at keeping germs out — unless you get a hole in them.

1. Find two apples that have no cuts, scrapes or bruises.

2. Wash your hands, and then both apples, with soap.

3. Place each apple on its own clean plate or piece of paper.

4. Ask an adult to carefully cut three or four dime-sized patches of skin from one apple.

5. Ask someone who hasn't just washed his hands to rub them all over the uncut apple, then all over the one with the cuts.

6. Leave both apples out for one week.

The cuts let in air, which turns the cuts brown. They probably also let in germs that begin to eat away the apple. Peel the uncut apple. You should find that none of the germs got through the skin to damage it. Like the apple skin, as long as yours is in one piece, it keeps the germs outside, where they belong.

Marvelous Mucus

Don't pick your nose! You know you shouldn't, but sometimes there's stuff in there that drives you nuts. That stuff is mucus, and that irritating booger is a sign that your immune system is doing its job.

The inside skin—called the mucus membrane—of your nose and your throat, too, makes nearly 250 mL (1 c.) of that slippery, sticky snot every single day. When you breathe in, any dust, germs, pollen and other stuff get stuck to the mucus. If they didn't, they could go sailing down to your lungs and cause you serious breathing trouble.

Once a germ or a bit of dust gets trapped in the mucus, it's stuck in your nose. You might get rid of it when you blow your nose. It might make you sneeze to send it flying. Or it might stay there until the mucus around it dries up into an annoying chunk that you want desperately to get rid of. But do everybody around you a favor—use a tissue.

- Hippopotamuses have mucus that's pink and oozes from their skin. Not only does it keep their skin from drying out, but it also contains a natural sunscreen, as well as a substance that kills germs.

- When a frog zaps its tongue out to catch a tasty morsel, glands in the tip produce sticky mucus that latches onto dinner and pulls it back in. If the glands produced sticky mucus all the time, the frog's mouth would be stuck shut.

- Healthy mucus is clear. Mucus filled with viruses or bacteria is cloudy or might even be yellow or — ugh — green.

You Try It

Mix up a batch of fake snot to explore the stretchiness and sliminess of mucus — without the gross-out factor.

1. Mix 1.25 mL (1/4 tsp.) of Borax laundry booster with 45 mL (3 tbsp.) of warm water.

2. Stir until most of the powder has dissolved. Let the mixture cool.

3. Squirt 15 mL (1 tbsp.) of white glue into a small bowl.

4. Add 15 mL (1 tbsp.) of water. Mix together well.

5. Add 10 mL (2 tsp.) of the laundry booster mixture to the glue. Stir. You should get a lump of fake snot in a puddle of cloudy water.

Quickly remove some snot from the container. Is it stretchy and slimy? That's what makes mucus perfect for trapping particles so they can't get past your nose. Remember: this snot DOES NOT belong in your nose. Be sure to throw your fake snot in the trash and wash your hands.

Germ Warfare

In the late 1980s, Dr. Greg Bossart noticed a pattern. As a veterinarian at the Miami Seaquarium, he treated sick and injured sea animals from both inside the aquarium and out. People often brought him wild manatees with terrible wounds from boat propellers, wounds that the vet knew would probably be so seriously infected the animal would die. Yet somehow the manatees almost always survived.

Why are manatees so resilient? It's because of their blood. Like people and other mammals, manatees have white blood cells in their blood that help protect against infection and disease. Dr. Bossart discovered that manatees have a higher number of an important type called lymphocytes (LIM-fo-sites), and 90 percent of those are T helpers—cells that are crucial in fighting disease and infection.

Most other mammals have fewer lymphocytes than manatees, and in people, just 60 percent of lymphocytes are T helpers. Studying the manatee's strong immune system may help doctors find better ways to treat people with immune-system diseases such as lupus, leukemia or AIDS.

- A drop of your blood holds between 150,000 and 450,000 white blood cells.

- As you get older, your body can recognize more viruses and fight them off better. Children average 6 to 10 colds each year. Adults get only 2 to 4.

How Your Body Fights Back

Even though your body is protected by your skin, ear wax, nose hairs and mucus, germs do get through. So other parts of your immune system are always on guard. A fist-sized organ called the spleen sits just behind your stomach and filters your blood to remove bacteria. Your blood looks for invading germs, too.

"Natural killer cells" in your blood kill cells that have been taken over by viruses. Other blood cells — macrophages (MAK-row-faj-ez) and dendritic cells — spot unusual germs or cells and show them to T helpers (the ones manatees have so many of) and to other lymphocytes called B cells and T killer cells.

The B cells recognize any dangerous germs and produce an antibody, a kind of marker, that sticks to the foreign germs. Once the bad cells are marked, macrophages and other cells can recognize them as bad for you and kill them.

If the T killer cells recognize the invaded cells shown to them as something bad, they kill them. The T helpers signal the T killer cells to multiply, making more cells that can recognize and kill cells taken over by this virus. The extra T killer cells are produced in the lymph nodes or glands. It's these extra cells that make your glands swell up when you're sick.

Once the immune cells in your body recognize what they're fighting, the battle is almost over. And your body remembers the bad guys for your entire life. If the same kind of germ ever tries to invade your body again, your white blood cells will recognize it and kill it before it has a chance to reproduce and make you sick.

Hot Under the Collar

Thousands of years ago, surgeons in ancient Babylon didn't have the tools today's doctors have. Instead of X-rays and ultrasounds to help them find what was making a patient sick, they had their own technology — mud.

The surgeons would cover the patient in wet clay and watch to see what part dried fastest. That's where they would make the first cut, hoping to find the problem. Amazingly, many times they did.

These long-ago doctors had noticed something that all modern doctors know: if part of you gets sick, it usually gets hot. And when your whole body is fighting off bacteria or viruses, your cells send a chemical "Help!" message to your brain. The brain then cranks up your body temperature by a few degrees. The fever kills off the bacteria and keeps viruses from reproducing so quickly. Fewer bacteria or viruses mean you get better faster.

That's why all you have to do is moan, "I don't feel very good," and before you can say "thermometer," somebody's stuck one under your tongue. Taking your temperature doesn't help you get better, but it can let people know if your body really is sick.

Fever Frenzy

A fever can be scary, especially for parents of a sick child. They know a really high fever can cause brain damage. If a fever is dangerously high, doctors sometimes prescribe medicine to lower it. Other times, they say it's best to leave a fever alone. By allowing your body to raise its temperature (but not too much), you let it do its job and fight whatever germs are trying to settle in.

- **The old advice "Feed a cold but starve a fever" may be correct. A study shows that eating food increases the immune response your body uses to fight a virus such as one that causes a cold, while not eating increases the response that fights bacteria and the fever they often cause.**

You Try It

When you have a fever, you don't always feel hot. Lots of times you get chills that make you shiver. That's because the air around you now feels so much cooler compared with your skin. Warm water can show you how this works.

1. Fill a large bowl with lukewarm water.

2. Fill a second bowl with water about as hot as a bath or shower.

3. Place one hand in the lukewarm water and your other hand in the hot water for at least 30 seconds.

4. Move the hand that's in hot water to the lukewarm water. Does the temperature feel the same to both hands?

The hand that first heated up in the hot water likely feels cool because the lukewarm water is so much cooler. When you have a fever, your super-hot skin makes the regular air around you seem much cooler, too. Brr!

Under the Weather

On February 21, 1990, NASA was preparing for the next day's launch of the space shuttle ATLANTIS when it ran into a problem. Astronaut John Creighton had a sore throat and a runny nose. He'd caught a plain old, everyday cold virus. It delayed the launch for a week, and cost NASA an extra $2.5 million. Talk about an expensive cold!

- In spite of what your parents say, you can't catch a cold by standing in the rain or not wearing a hat. Only a virus can cause a cold. Getting cold and wet might affect how well you fight off a virus you already have, though.

- You'll never pass your cold onto Fido or Fluffy. The cold viruses that make us sick don't affect dogs and cats. And the viruses that give THEM cold symptoms don't affect us.

When a Cold Takes Hold

You know that feeling. Your head seems heavy, achy and full of fluff. Your throat's sore, especially when you cough, which is all the time. When your nose isn't busy sneezing, it's running. And all you want to do is sleep. Welcome to the world of the common cold. The strange thing is that none of these symptoms is caused by the viruses that are invading you. What makes you feel so crummy is your body trying to fight back.

Once the viruses get into your breathing passages, they take over cells there to make copies of themselves. Your body sends more blood to repair the injured cells and battle the viruses. It's that extra blood, not the viruses or their damage, that makes your throat and the lining of your nose and sinuses swollen and painful.

Your body also makes lots more mucus to trap the viruses in your nose and sinuses and flush them out of your body. That's what gives you your runny nose and stuffed-up head. And since your body's working hard to do all this, it needs tons of extra sleep to keep up, which is why when you're sick you have about as much energy as a soggy noodle.

Fighting a cold can be a nuisance, but if your body didn't do it, those tiny cold viruses could eventually kill you.

You Try It

Not all colds cause exactly the same set of symptoms. The next time someone in your family comes down with one, keep track of how the cold progresses. Ask the patient questions such as:

- Did it start as a sore throat?
- Was there a cough?
- On what day of the cold did your nose begin to run?
- Did the sore throat get better partway through the cold?

If someone else gets sick, keep track of that new patient's symptoms. If the symptoms follow the same pattern, it could mean both people are sick from the same virus.

Pain in the Neck

Away back in about the year 40, a surgeon named Celsus was looking at a patient's sore throat. He saw two swollen red lumps of tissue, one on each side of the throat.

Like other surgeons at that time, Celsus had no idea what was causing the sore throat. But he decided to get rid of the swollen stuff by cutting the lumps out, performing what was probably the world's first tonsillectomy. Doctors have been removing tonsils ever since.

Viruses love your throat because, like your other breathing passages, it's the perfect temperature for viruses to reproduce in. That's where your tonsils come in. Tonsils are large lymph nodes in your throat. Like your other lymph nodes, the tonsils swell up when they're busy making extra lymphocytes to fight off an invasion of germs.

Doctors used to think that tonsils were useful only in fighting germs in young children. They now believe tonsils may fight germs your whole life—unless they've been taken out. Some people's tonsils get swollen and infected so often that they cause other problems and have to be removed.

- When you cough, your body pushes out air at the speed of sound, about 1,225 km/h (760 m.p.h.).

- In the early 1900s, many doctors thought removing anyone's tonsils would make that person healthier. In some cities, they removed the tonsils of every child who was in public school. Now doctors perform a tonsillectomy only on a patient who needs it.

Ahem!

People often call coughing "clearing your throat," and that's exactly what it is. Germs, bits of dust, a piece of food, a glob of mucus—any of these things can bother your throat's lining. That triggers a reflex that makes you take a deep breath, narrow your throat and blast out air and whatever else is in there. (Be sure to aim for your sleeve or a tissue so you won't spread germs around.)

Sometimes, though, it's the swollen, irritated lining itself that triggers the reflex. That's why, when you're sick, you may seem to cough and cough. People have been known to cough so hard they break a rib.

You Try It

The next time you have a sore throat, try eating or drinking one of these:

- a Popsicle
- hot tea
- apple juice
- chicken soup

Which of them made your throat feel better? All liquids (even frozen ones) are good for you, but the cold foods can numb the sore area a little and may ease the pain. And if your doctor tells you there are bacteria down there, skip the sweets and eat something salty instead. Salt kills bacteria, but sugar feeds them.

The Flu

It's March of 1919. The Montreal Canadiens are battling the Seattle Metropolitans for the Stanley Cup. Each hockey team has won two games and tied one. The tie-breaking game is set for April 1, but the game's never played. History records no Stanley Cup champion that year. What could possibly have canceled that all-important final game? A war? An earthquake? Believe it or not, it was the flu.

Soldiers returning home from Europe after the end of World War I in 1918 unknowingly brought along a terrible influenza (or flu) virus known as the Spanish flu. It infected more than half a BILLION people around the world — that was 1 in every 10 people alive — and killed many of them.

People tried their best to stop it from spreading. Cinemas, theaters and churches were closed, and public meetings and sports events were canceled. Many cities passed a law that everyone had to wear a surgical mask. Even shaking hands was illegal.

When it was all over, the flu had killed nearly 40 million people worldwide — more than twice as many people as had died in World War I.

Another Virus

The flu's a lot like a cold. Both are caused by a virus that settles in your breathing passages. They spread the same way, through the air or by people touching germ-covered surfaces, then rubbing their nose or eyes. And both of them usually start with a sore throat. A lot of the other symptoms may be the same too: stuffed-up nose, cough, headache and feeling tired. When you have the flu, though, the symptoms are usually worse. The sore throat's sorer, your head's more stuffed up and the whole thing nearly always lasts longer.

There are three "families," or types, of flu viruses. Type A flu is the most serious and the type that causes worldwide epidemics such as the Spanish flu epidemic. Type B is similar but not as common. Type C is even less common, and its symptoms are milder.

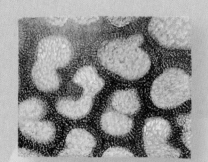

Type A flu

Sick as a ... Horse?

People aren't the only animals that get the flu. Birds, pigs, ducks, whales, horses and seals can all catch some Type A flu bugs. In fact, animals can even give the flu to people. Researchers believe the Spanish flu of 1918 and the swine flu of 1976 both came from pigs. And in 1998, people caught Avian flu from chickens.

- What people call the stomach flu isn't a flu. It's an infection of the stomach and intestines by another kind of virus. Flu viruses infect only breathing passages.

- The flu has been making people sick for more than 1,500 years. In 412 B.C., the Greek doctor Hippocrates wrote about an illness that, according to today's doctors and historians, sounds just like influenza.

From Bad to Worse

For most people, a cold or a bout of the flu means a week or so of lying in bed, achy and bored. After that, your body rallies and you get better. Sometimes, though, a cold or flu can turn into something more serious.

If it spreads from your throat and sinuses to other parts of your breathing passages, that part of you gets sick. Viruses in the bronchial tubes— air passages connected to your lungs—can give you bronchitis, and the sore throat and serious breathing troubles that come with it. Or a virus might get into your lungs themselves. Then you'd have viral pneumonia.

When viruses find their way to your voice box, or larynx, you'll probably get laryngitis. They can even get into the passageways that lead to your ears and give you a nasty earache.

The Terrible Twosome

Dealing with a virus can be tough, but it gets even tougher when bacteria show up on the scene as well. All that extra fluid and congestion in your stuffy nose and other passages can clog them up for days. That means the few bacteria that would normally drain out get the chance to hang around and reproduce instead. Then what started as a virus gets complicated by a bacterial infection.

Ear infections, sinus infections, bacterial pneumonia — all these can be a lot harder to fight, especially when your body's already worn out from battling the virus you got in the first place.

You've Got WHAT in Your Ears?

Never stick anything in your ear. It's a good rule, but sometimes doctors have to break it. Some kids get frequent ear infections and have lots of trouble getting rid of them. Those kids may have to have surgery to put tiny tubes in their ears.

Each tube fits into a little hole a surgeon makes in the eardrum. The tube lets fluid, bacteria and other gunk drain from the middle ear more easily, to help the patient get better. Usually, in six months or so, the eardrum heals itself, squeezing out the tube in the process. By then, the patient's usually over the worst of the infection.

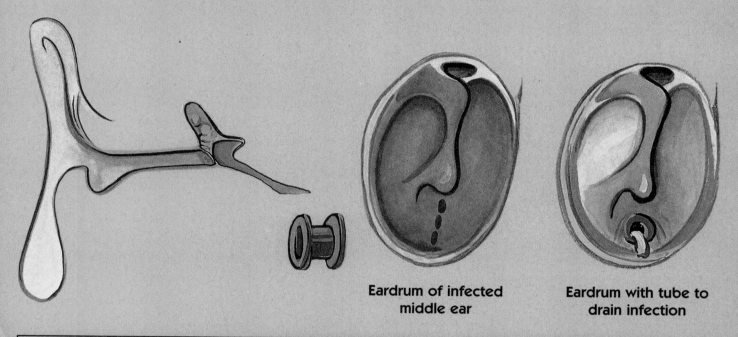

Eardrum of infected middle ear

Eardrum with tube to drain infection

- Bacterial pneumonia can be very contagious, and not just for people. Pigs get pneumonia, too, which is bad news for pig farmers. Believe it or not, pigs cough and sneeze the same as people do, sending their germs flying far and wide and spreading the pneumonia to the other pigs around them.

On the Mend

In 1928, a researcher named Alexander Fleming made an incredible discovery completely by accident. He was studying bacteria, trying to figure out what could kill them. Before he went on holiday, he smeared bacteria onto some agar, a sort of jelly the bacteria could eat, then forgot to cover the experiment. While he was gone, a spore from a mold called **Penicillium** drifted through his window and into the experiment.

Two weeks later, Fleming could see that his bacteria had spread all over the agar — except where the mold had formed. He'd discovered a mold that could kill bacteria. Through more experiments, he found the lethal substance that the mold produced. He called the world's first bacteria-killer, or antibiotic, penicillin.

It was many years before two other scientists, Howard Florey and Ernst Chain, did more experiments and showed the world how important penicillin could be. Finally, in about 1941, doctors had a medicine to treat bacterial pneumonia, diphtheria, scarlet fever and other bacterial illnesses that had killed so many people. Penicillin also saved the lives of thousands of soldiers wounded on the battlefield during World War II.

Making Bacteria Sick

When bacteria come across **Penicillium** mold and try to gobble it up, the mold does what any creature would do: protect itself. It produces a kind of poison. It's this poison that people call penicillin and use as an antibiotic. If you have a bacterial infection, your doctor can prescribe penicillin to kill the bacteria inside you without hurting any of your healthy cells.

Researchers have found and developed other antibiotics, too. Some of these don't kill the bacteria, but instead stop them from growing and spreading, so your body has a chance to kill them off.

- The fluids in your body, such as your tears and saliva, contain something called lysozyme. It acts like a weak antibiotic and can kill bacteria if there are only a few of them.

- Hundreds of years before Fleming studied **Penicillium** mold, Mayan Indians in Central America were making a bacteria-fighting medicine from moldy roasted corn.

You Try It

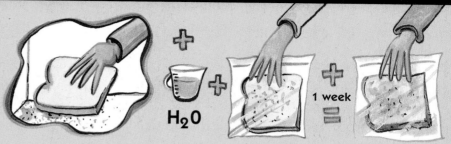

You can grow your very own crop of **Penicillium** mold, but just to look at, not to eat. Penicillin, the medicine, has been processed and sterilized to make it safe. The stuff you're going to grow hasn't.

1. Rub a slice of bread on a dusty corner of the counter or floor.

2. Sprinkle a little water onto the bread to dampen it. Then seal it inside a resealable plastic bag.

3. Place the bag in a warm, dark place and leave it for a week.

4. Check the bread. DO NOT OPEN THE BAG.

See any green, furry-looking patches on your bread? If so, congratulations. You've just grown **Penicillium** mold. Have a good look, then throw the bread away, still sealed inside the bag.

Speedy Recovery

In 1799, George Washington, the president of the United States, died of a cold—sort of. He caught a cold virus, and his doctors began working hard to "cure" him.

They made Washington gargle with a mixture of molasses, vinegar and butter. Then they placed some goop made from dried beetles on his throat. And finally, the doctors cut him four times to bleed out the poisons they thought were making him sick. Washington died within three days—not from the cold, but from the "cures."

Even now, more than two hundred years later, doctors wouldn't be able to make Washington's cold go away. Antibiotics are amazing at fighting bacteria, but they do absolutely nothing against viruses. That's why taking penicillin won't help your cold. It takes time for your body to battle a cold or flu virus and get back in control. So the most important thing doctors prescribe is rest.

There ARE some things you can do to feel better, though. Cold medicines from the pharmacy can stop the coughing or clear a stuffed-up head. Gargling with warm, salty water can help a sore throat. Turning on a vaporizer at night can help, too. It keeps the lining of your nose moist so it won't dry out and crack, giving germs another way into your body.

Grandma's Chicken Soup

Of all the remedies that people have tried over thousands of years to help people with colds feel better, it turns out that chicken soup may be just about the best. People have been using it as medicine since the 12th century.

Doctors know that drinking lots of fluids helps a cold, and they know that warm liquids act like a fever to raise your body temperature and slow down the virus. But chicken soup seems to help even more than that, and doctors can't explain why.

In one experiment, researchers gave one group of cold-sufferers plenty of cold water. They gave a second group the same amount of hot water, and gave a third group hot chicken soup. The people who drank the chicken soup got much more relief of their cold symptoms, especially congestion, than any of the others.

- A Roman writer two thousand years ago wrote that you could cure a cold by "kissing the hairy muzzle of a mouse."

- In the United States, more chicken soup is sold in January, at the height of the cold and flu season, than at any other time of the year.

For Coughs & Colds

Keeping the Germs Away

How would you like to risk your life to end one of the world's most deadly diseases? That's what eight-year-old James Phipps did. In the 1700s, smallpox was a very dangerous sickness. Almost everyone caught it, and one-third of them died from it. But in 1796, an English country doctor named Edward Jenner found a way to prevent people from catching it.

For hundreds of years, country people had said that milkmaids who caught a harmless sickness called vaccinia (VAK-sin-ya) — or cowpox — from the cows they milked never got smallpox. So Dr. Jenner rubbed some pus from a milkmaid who had cowpox into cuts on the arm of healthy James Phipps.

When the boy had gotten over the cowpox, Dr. Jenner infected him with smallpox. It was a dangerous experiment — James could easily have died. Luckily, the experiment worked. Jenner had just completed the world's first vaccination.

How Vaccination Works

Some viruses or bacteria reproduce so quickly your immune system can't keep up. It takes time to recognize the germ, get the word out all over your body and make extra white blood cells for the battle. By then, the infection has practically taken over.

A vaccination gives your body a head start. The doctor injects fluid, called a vaccine, that contains bacteria or viruses of the sickness. The germs have been disabled — either killed, weakened or cut up into pieces — so that the vaccine won't give you the illness. Once the germs are in you, your immune system can make its preparations. Then, if that sickness ever makes it into your body, your immune system's ready.

Today, there are more than 20 different vaccines to protect people, especially children, from viruses and bacteria that cause diseases such as polio, diphtheria, tetanus and mumps. Even pets get vaccinated — against rabies.

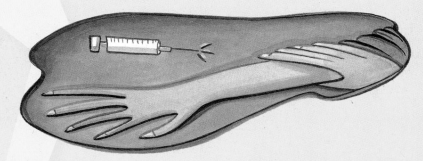

Flu Vaccines

Doctors now have vaccines to protect people from some types of flu. The trouble is that flu viruses can change as they travel around from person to person. The flu vaccine you got this year will protect you from one type of flu, but once that flu changes, your body won't recognize it anymore.

Germkillers

Scientists have created a number of different products to fight germs before they can get inside you. Antiseptics — those things you pour on a scrape — wash away many bacteria and weaken the ones left behind so they can't grow.

Disinfectants battle germs, too, by killing them or keeping them from growing. Certain disinfectants, called viricides (VY-ri-sides), can kill viruses. Lots of these products work well, but you can use them only to wipe off tables, counters and other objects. If they got into you, they'd kill off all your healthy cells along with the germs.

Healthy Future

In 1964, a man named Norman Cousins became very sick. Lying in a hospital bed, he was in so much pain that even sleeping was difficult for him. Then one day he watched a comedy video. His pain dulled and he fell asleep.

Norman tried it a few more times and discovered that laughing, even just for a couple of minutes, could help him get two hours of pain-free sleep. He felt it was helping him get better, too. Eventually, Norman completely recovered from his sickness — he says, because of laughter.

Not all doctors agree that laughter cured Norman Cousins, but some researchers have found that a hearty laugh can actually increase the germ-fighting cells in a person's immune system. Future research may show that laughter can help keep sickness away and even help patients with long-term illnesses feel better.

Mind Over Matter

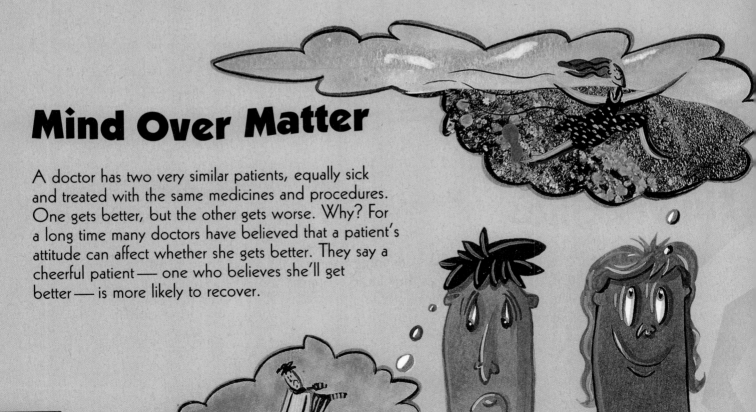

A doctor has two very similar patients, equally sick and treated with the same medicines and procedures. One gets better, but the other gets worse. Why? For a long time many doctors have believed that a patient's attitude can affect whether she gets better. They say a cheerful patient — one who believes she'll get better — is more likely to recover.

Germs in the 21st Century

Since 1850, doctors and scientists have made huge leaps in understanding germs, fighting the bad ones and using the good ones. Antibiotics, vaccines and keeping things clean have saved more people than you can imagine. Many once-deadly diseases are now easily treated, and mostly prevented. Smallpox, which has killed millions of people since it was first recognized in 1157, has been completely wiped out.

Scientists may know a lot about the human immune system, but there are still mysteries to be solved. Perhaps, one day, there will be cures for the flu, the common cold and every other illness. Or doctors might discover germs that are more difficult to fight. Maybe, in the future, people won't even get sick. One thing's certain: No matter what medicines are invented, none of them will do as much to keep you healthy as your incredible immune system.

- Someday, just a glance at your bandaged cut may be enough to tell you if it's infected. Researchers are developing bandage strips that change color if there's an infection underneath. The color the bandage becomes will even tell your doctor what type of bacterium is growing there.

Index